The Secretary Parables

The Secretary Parables

by Nancy Lagomarsino

Alice James Books

Cambridge, Massachusetts

Grateful acknowledgement is made

to the following publications in which versions of the following poems

first appeared: *Calliope* ("Finale"); *Cimarron Review* ("Lost Years," "Shadows," "The

Tiger," "The Years with Small Children"); *Great River Review* ("The Wedding"); *The*

Louisville Review ("The Ballet," "Early Ruin," "Stories from Life"); *Ploughshares* ("On

Skimming an Anthology of Contemporary American Poetry," "400 Yard Girls'

Relay"); *Quarterly West* ("Duration"); *The Poetry Miscellany* ("Descent").

Library of Congress Cataloging-in-Publication Data

Lagomarsino, Nancy.

The secretary parables / by Nancy Lagomarsino

I. Title

PS3562.A3128S4   1991   811'.54--dc20   91-16373

ISBN 0-914086-92-8

Cover Drawing by Robina MacIntyre

Book Design and Typesetting by William Lach

Printed by Evans Printing Company, Concord, New Hampshire

Alice James Books gratefully acknowledges

support from the National Endowment for the Arts and from the Massachusetts

Council on the Arts and Humanities, a state agency whose funds are recommended

by the Governor and appropriated by the State Legislature.

Alice James Books are published by the Alice James Poetry Cooperative, Inc.

Alice James Books, 33 Richdale Avenue, Cambridge, Massachusetts 02140

This book

is dedicated to

Dorothy Amelia Beck

(1928 - 1989)

source of

immeasurable strength

Contents

Rescue

Duration

Duration

... Instead of countries and rivers, a globe that maps out time. A shape something like the Americas for the two World Wars, linked by an isthmus of peace. A blotch of mustard yellow for the Reformation. A latitude and longitude for every moment past and future, and, at the two poles, the moment that is happening and its opposite.

Oceans separate the great events, galleons founder, and the wind circles, looking for the pine tree where it was born.

This globe balances on a dresser in a child's bedroom. In the top drawer, her underwear and pajamas. Then, a drawer of shirts, shorts, pants. At the bottom, scarves, mittens, a jumble of stored winter clothes. It is summer, the long vacation ... on the globe, a snaking blue line.

Treadwell Street

I was so happy to be in first grade — at share time I stood and sang *The Aba Daba Honeymoon*, a cheerful tune about a monkey and a chimp who were married by a baboon.

Halfway through the year they promoted me to second grade. I took my art folder and walked down the hall to Miss McVery's room. I got along fine in reading, but I couldn't figure out second grade arithmetic, no matter how much tutoring I got. After school I was shown movies of balls being added to other balls and then subtracted. Two and three columns of balls swimming on the screen. After a month, I was handed my art folder and send back to first grade.

Later at home my mother comforted me. She told me a story about a boy who skipped three grades. He ended up so lonely, he ran away. "Be glad you're not brilliant," she said.

The Baby Sitter

Can you keep a secret? he whispered. Then he offered me a dollar if I would pull down my underpants when he pulled down his. I must have been six or seven, and he was in college. I can't remember the rest very well.

I'm careful not to let my sons see me undressed. Some mothers are more relaxed, but I've always been modest, and my sons are modest. Of course when they were babies it was different — at night I moved nakedly from my husband to the crib, lifted a baby into my arms and held him against my breasts. Or I sat in the bath with a baby, and the baby was glad.

I have an ordinary body, yet when I look at myself with the eyes of a child I'm surprised by the hair. It's the first thing I see.

The Tiger

Not far from my grandparents' house lived one tiger, the most solitary of the cats in Forest Park Zoo, his roar the most heartfelt. He looked through the bars the way I looked through the screens on our porch, not with hope or interest, but in resignation, that ledge we come to during a steep climb. In the tiger's case, he had climbed down from his own life into one envisioned by his keeper; in my case, I was climbing up toward a life there was no need to envision, so similar was it to the lives around me.

Though we were climbing in different directions, the tiger and I had much in common — I, too, was solitary, and my passion sat near me like an untouched water dish. I paced the porch mat, watched cars and sometimes disappeared into the house, just as the tiger sometimes disappeared into an inner chamber. The difference was, people waited for him to show himself, whereas no one waited for me, unless you count each car as a person, and the shadow behind each car as the car's effort to wait.

Men Who Work Hard

I think of my grandfather as a shadow, perhaps because of the gray felt hat and topcoat he wore downstreet every day. There is something indistinct about men who work hard. Their families wait for them to come home, and in this way children learn to wait.

He was city treasurer, but his real love was photography. As a shadow would, he held up his light meter to measure our light. *Watch how fast I can run!* I called, and his camera followed me, but it couldn't convey my speed.

At his funeral, the casket was left open. He looked asleep, in one of his gray suits. This was the first death to touch me, a dream from early in the night.

400 Yard Girls' Relay

I was the first and slowest man — for that sort of thing, you called yourself a man. I handed the baton to Rae, who passed it to Sue, and on to Sharlene. We were the four best runners among the girls in the senior class.

Rae got married after high school and had kids. Sue left college to get married and also had kids. Both are divorced now. I don't know what happened to Sharlene, but she had a wild streak. I wish I knew her address.

I was voted "the girl who gets away with the most." I never felt I got away with anything. True, I refused to write an in-class English theme for Mr. Hatch. He called me "the girl who thinks she's too good for high school." I didn't think that. I thought I hated writing. Even now I think words are batons passed between men.

Practice Flight

After school, I faced my dreams the way plants face light. I slept in a room with flowered wallpaper and a braided rug I was taught to vacuum in circles.

In one dream, I was part of a mutiny at the back of a classroom. Our leader went up to argue with the teacher, and on her way back to her seat she opened her arms and soared through the air. With a kind of mental thrashing I tried to copy her, but in my effort to steer I was swept outside toward some power lines. Before I could cry out, the heavy cords brushed my back.

Sometimes it's hard to know if a dream is over, whether we've woken too soon. I wasn't meant to touch the lines. This dream ended because I did.

The Ballet

I've never been to the ballet, but this is how I imagine it ... I go alone and surrender my wrap. The velvet curtain rises.

It's not a feminist ballet — the hero soars, the heroine doesn't soar unless lifted by a man with bulging tights. Is it enough to be supremely graceful, tossed about like a garland?

I'm reminded of the time in high school when I wanted to be an airline hostess tottering on spikes in some exotic bazaar. I didn't want to be a nurse, a teacher, or a secretary-receptionist. I wanted to balance turbulent trays and marry a pilot.

One Christmas my mother gave me a jewelry box. Every time I opened the lid, a delicate ballerina spun to music. I kept my teapot pin in there, my wooden N hanging by a chain, the snake bracelet Dick gave me. When I lay in bed at night, the ballerina was company. She did nothing but sleep among my jewels or dance, yet I never thought to condemn her.

Early Ruin

When I met with my therapist, I often ran into the woman whose appointment was scheduled just before mine. As I entered the waiting room, she would be shrugging on her coat, or closing an inner door behind her. My mind would be full of dream fragments, because I believed that dreams conceal clues.

The therapist was an unsmiling man from the Freudian school. Since I had tried to take my life, I was forbidden to go on dates or trips without permission. He warned that if I disobeyed him, he would sign papers to commit me.

I remember all this now with a shrug, the shrug everyone gives when there are no words. I can tell you about my life and its restrictions, I can mention the waiting room, the woman I never tried to know. I can tell you that after a few months I left therapy without permission.

But there are no words to describe how I felt. Dreams are saturated with feelings, but you can't wring them out. You ruin your life, or you don't. You promise not to take death lightly. You promise this to someone you know you will never see again. You wear a scarf to therapy, and you untie it from your neck.

Anouilh's *Antigone*

Twenty-five years later, I have a chance to see the play I'd once starred in. Young women are still auditioning for doomed heroine — it's considered a strong part. I watch this actress go through a modern dress version with no break, and I can't believe I memorized so many lines. I can't believe how tedious the arguments are, how stiff the words.

In the dark theater I close my eyes and conjure up my jade silk costume that draped to the floor. No one notices how my face softens when I slip into my long ago body. I mean to interfere with myth, to become Antigone again and vow to live.

Lost Years

In Greece, families keep their daughters behind walls,
weapons sensed but not seen. I, too, was raised to be striking
— I could be a stone to strike men.

I wanted that. I posed, I was artless. It never occurred to
me to hold the camera, to think of myself as a writer.

I should have forgotten men. I married a poet, and like a
fool I ironed his pillowcase.

In Greece, most women my age wear black. There is
dignity in black, the dignity of loss. I think I could talk with
these women. Then I think, no.

Boston Tea Party, 1967

I marched with the grape pickers past secretaries straggling
back from lunch, through the financial district and down the
old streets to the harbor. I felt useful, arm-in-arm with men
from the vineyards. I kept glancing at the secretaries — I could
have admitted *I'm a secretary too* and handed them bouquets
of grapes, but that was before I cared about other women. I
cared about migrant workers, segregation, Vietnam, but back
then no one I knew marched for women. The secretaries
vanished into their buildings, and we handed our grapes to the
sea.

Finale

All night I trapeze above the husband in my bed and the stranger in my dreams. Miles apart, both men sleep lightly, arms spread wide on sheets taut as safety nets, anxious crowds murmuring in their throats. In that split second while my body decides to go no higher, I look at the one below me, his eyeglasses balanced on tired hands, and I think, *that is my husband*, or *that is the other one*, in his namelessness more powerful, like the shy acrobat who finishes with the whole troupe on his shoulders.

How can I stay still down where I'm wanted? And what do *I* want, besides men? Besides the bodies of sleeping men, innocent in spangles and tights? Never mind, as long as someone's ready when I plummet from the top of the tent. It's part of the act to need someone that much.

Journeys

You wake up enough to say, *I'll sleep a little longer.*

I lie next to you and read while the sky lightens, brew coffee, come back to bed and read some more, a book of firsthand accounts by trauma victims who ventured a short way into death.

Your face on the pillow alters, though your eyes are closed. You could be dreaming about your waking life, or about a dream you had when you were more deeply asleep.

I touch your shoulder, as I sometimes touch the shoulder of a friend I won't see for a while.

The Hunters

October sunlight streams through windows propped open. I'm in a dream your touching brought on ... a rustling so far within me only I can hear it. You are the hunter after pheasant, your pointer perfectly trained.

Now it's my turn to be the hunter. I hunt without a gun. The dog I use whimpers. We follow the ravine that leads to Needle Rock. The pheasant hides in you.

The Wedding

We can't see much from the balcony, the bride's floral headpiece, the groom's bald spot. Their children from past marriages crowd into the front row, close enough to hear every promise.

Secretly I wonder why she's marrying again, even as I join with my husband in the common prayer. Shouldn't she kick off her taffeta shoes and race back into the parking lot? One of the cars would have keys. One of the empty houses would take her in.

On the way home, we stop for dinner and eavesdrop on conversations around us, having exhausted our own on the journey here. You propose a toast — *to us* — and our eyes meet. At the next table, a couple is arguing about a separation. They seem to be trying to smash a plank of silence, the same silence that both links and divides us.

I'm still trying to understand what married love means, how we discard it temporarily, and how we get it back.

The Years with Small Children

On the beach, a young woman lies flat in her maternity bathing suit while two children bury her with sand. The older child tells her not to move ... if she moves, she'll spoil it. The younger one mixes cement.

The time with small children weighs on some of us like sand patted down. Years later, we can still feel the grit, the heaviness that slows our steps when a child holds on to our life. We trudge through the sand to a good spot, scoop water onto our shoulders, we brush ourselves off at the end of the day, we stoop. One year the water is fresh, another, salt. We look forward to burial as a time of rest. We seek out a child and ask to be buried. The child makes sand pillows for our heads.

Rafflesia arnoldii

Peter is recovering in his room. He won't let anyone look at the coarse black threads stitched among the hairs of his eyebrow, where the hardball cracked his skull.

Just hours ago, he and I were soaking up his blood with gauze squares while we waited in the clinic. All the blood that had left my face seemed to be pouring out of his. *National Geographic* lurked by every lamp — I knew Peter felt he'd already studied nature at school, but I thought we both might be distracted by an article about the largest flower in the world … not really a flower, more a parasite nearly a yard wide that blossoms and rots in Sumatra. As I got deeper, I tried to downplay the part about how carrion flies are its chief pollinators, lured by a smell of decaying flesh. I skipped over how short a time it blossoms, and how some call it the "stinking corpse lily." Instead, I emphasized the flower's magnificence, its weight of fifteen pounds, its mysterious origin in the jungle floor. It takes nine months from bud to flower, just like a person!

Peter looked at the pictures with eyes tangled in disinterest. Where's your sense of humor? I said. Then the doctor came in, and I shrank far enough into the shadows to be of help.

August 15

Today Jeremy turns sixteen. We were living in England when he was born, and we gave him three names — Jeremy for a liberal politician we admired, David for his father, and Owen for Wilfred Owen, a World War I poet who died in battle. The first two names would have been enough.

For the past few weeks we've been practicing his driving over at the cemetery, where the roads are quiet. Mr. Tanzi has a natural boulder for a gravestone. I told Jeremy I'd like something along that line, and he shifted gears. It's strange having a child in the driver's seat, but I don't get as nervous as I thought I would. Jeremy's careful. The other day he passed through the cemetery gates and onto a living road.

Baby Ding

When my children were small, and the house full of Cheerios, I offered to take care of a six-month-old baby named Dinh. We called him Baby Ding.

He came to our house Monday through Friday, 8-5, an impassive baby with a chronic stuffy nose. His young parents had left Vietnam in boats, different boats in different directions. They finally found one another at a refugee camp in Florida and travelled north to start a new life. The baby was born here, when they had no money.

I wanted to help, to make up as best I could for the children caught in Vietnam. But Baby Ding never smiled or tried to get around. I don't think there was anything wrong with him, he was just different from the babies I was used to. I brought him close to our trees, I carried him with me everywhere, and I encouraged the other children to play with him. He didn't seem to care about any of us. His parents became careless about picking him up on time, as if they were relaxing back into their lives.

After a few months they moved away to new jobs, and I never saw Baby Ding again. He was my only experience of Vietnam — sometimes I think of him, when I plunge into that thicket of those I meant to love.

The Choice

Her circumstance is so different from mine, she doesn't want a child right now. She would rather die than bring another child with its sand pail into this world.

I don't want her child either — my own children are oceans that surround me. To deny her is to refuse help to one who has drunk poison.

What of the unborn child?

Don't think of it as a child. If there's no other choice, think of it as a dream the body had.

Listen to the Dream

Years out of date, my dreams consider high school games, thermoses, opposing fans ... high in the stands, I drop my soda bottle through the slats and wait for the smash. Give me a W, Give me an E! How can I lure my dreams away from the simple rivalries of those early years and get them to help me with things as they are now?

A passing dream reins me in, saying — Don't try to outsmart your dreams. Think of dreams as music you can see.

Think of dreams as disorderly opera. You float above the stage, a slight feeling of heaviness in your legs. You don't recognize any of those singers, yet they belong near you.

Think of dreams as time spent learning a new piece. You announce, "I had a strange dream last night," but your family and friends had dreams of their own and don't really listen. You try to remember everything, exactly how the dream started, who you were with and how you moved together from one measure to the next.

Think of dreams as sheet music. You hear the notes with your eyes.

The Secretary Parables

The Secretary Loses Her Composure

While typing for a non-profit agency, the secretary finds a tick burrowed in her neck. She knows she's supposed to unscrew it, but she's unnerved. In one motion she takes the soft body between her forefinger and thumb and yanks.

The tick, as big as any she's taken from her dog's ears, lies stupefied on the blotter. The secretary consults her skull. Then, using two pencils, she lifts the tick and drops it into her ashtray. A lit match, a pop, and her blood flows among the ashes.

Dogs and Children

On days off, the secretary walks with her dog through the woods, and the dog runs ahead. The secretary is reminded of her children, how they ran ahead. Sometimes she hides from the dog, and he thunders up and down the path hunting for her. She crouches behind a stump, and the dog crashes through the underbrush, leaping and clawing at her shirt.

The secretary counts this as love-making. Board games, too, she counts as love-making, when adults and children sit around the board, as around a fire, and move pieces shaped like ancient cones. The board has places for home and places for finish, and the adults hope the children will win, but sometimes an adult can't help beating a child. The adult wants to throw the game into the fire, but the child loves the game, the painted cones, the chance to finish with home, and begs the adults to crouch down and stay.

The Secretary's Hobby

The secretary buys a homing pigeon and places it in her shed. Next morning, she takes the pigeon in the pickup, drives fifty miles, releases it and races back to wait. The pigeon is drawn to its new home as iron filings to a magnet.

One day, while the pigeon is on its way home, the secretary considers burning the shed. She's curious to see whether the pigeon will roost nearby or settle in the coals. She's interested in the strength of the pigeon's desire to stay home or to go home.

The secretary might increase the number of her pigeons and give them names. It's up to her.

The Women's Tent

The secretary sits on the toilet, a fresh tampax clamped
between her teeth. Swiftly she pulls out the used tampax,
wraps it in tissue and tucks it in the wastebasket safe from
notice. Then she inserts the replacement at an angle she
sometimes misjudges.

When she was younger, she wore a pad hooked to a belt
by netting. For years she wore those narrow pallets between
her legs, moving from one month to another like a nomad.

For years she's left no trace.

The Secretary Mows the Lawn

The secretary mows back and forth, and the grass blows away to the right. Sometimes she has to stop to save a toad or cricket struggling near the blade. She loves these dramatic rescues — hopefully someone would do the same for her.

She doesn't really believe a huge hand would scoop her up and place her over by the roses. In spite of all her powers, she doesn't know what to believe. She may have been helped many times and not have known. Every year she looks back upon her life as on a newly cut row.

The Crossing

The secretary finds an infant abandoned in an alley. The infant is swaddled in plastic wrap — someone felt that new things should be wrapped in plastic. The secretary takes the infant in her arms and listens to its heart. She tries to breathe life into it, as she used to do with her dolls, but the infant has grown stale the way loose bread does.

The secretary thinks of the mummies of children she has seen in museums, bodies bound with stained linen woven as rushes are woven into a basket. She once wrapped her own children in pastel squares of a certain size, until their necks rested on flannel stalks. She laid each one with its head touching the end of the cradle, so that it could imagine itself still inside her.

*

Lucid Dreamer

Where can the secretary find freedom, if not in her dreams? Every night she drifts underwater — her dreams are the huge rocks she locates with her feet. The depths have a quality of warmth about them, so that she no longer wonders as much about light. Her toe brushes moss, and instantly she sees a child she hasn't cared for enough. If she wanted to control her dream she could transform the child into her success, but, no matter how many fine children she dreams of later, there is always this child.

Leaving the Path

The secretary was born in a country where animals were
fashioned from glass, and milkmaids curtseyed on the mantel. I
once asked her to describe that life to me, but she said it
would be as easy for a poplar to describe the bank it clung to.

Her first husband came from that country. His father
sometimes struck him, and his mother covered the bruises with
long-sleeved jerseys. When she thinks of her first husband, she
thinks of striped jerseys fresh from the wash.

Time spent caring for others was time on the path, and she
has always liked to follow paths. But now she leaves the path,
first walking with it in her sight, then putting hemlocks and
other trees between her and the path, until she no longer has a
sense of exactly where the path is. The forest opens before
her, and she sinks down in a stripe of sunlight. She can always
find the path again, at the place where it leaves her life.

The Vase

When she dies, she would like to be cremated and her ashes placed, not in an urn, but in a vase that once held flowers. The vase should be slender, with a fluted mouth, gray-green, and painted with an old-fashioned scene, shade trees and a dusty road disappearing into the haze.

The vase should rest in a cherry cabinet with glass doors and shelves holding ballerinas. A piano should sit in the corner away from the fire. She won't be confined to the vase, any more than music is confined to the body of a piano. From time to time she'll pause to visit her ashes, just as now she sometimes opens the piano bench in search of sheet music from another age.

Rescue

Descent

I go into myself down a flight of stairs, each step invisible in the darkness. Perhaps it would be simpler if I jumped without caring what happened, as I'm tempted to do from any high place, a roof or the platform of a fire tower. No matter where I start, I feel I'm too high — bent over blank paper, my head falls forward, and somewhere in my mind I take on life, open the door and listen for water before beginning the long descent.

At the first river I swim neither with the current nor against it, and when I look back I sense my face watching me. I'm my own teacher, carrying myself aloft the way a flame is carried in a flood, and I'm my own sidekick, taking on menial work, the things I'm tired of doing for my family.

I get so weary that I drop the flame, and the water gasps. I may have written only a few phrases at the top of the page, but to write more I must conjure light from a hollow candle. *Help me*, I whisper, appealing to the part of myself I banished to this remote place, once I'd learned that a fiery nature is a kettle made of wood.

Writing for an Audience

As always, I want to share everything with you ... the path overgrown with goldenrod, brook trout nudging one another, and, to the north, a claybank thousands of years old, its slope littered with saplings, white pine and poplar rooted to thin air, as every year more clay washes away.

I hope you'll see things as I did. Out early on an unfamiliar path, I was ready to turn back when the steep bank emerged half in mist, tree limbs floating in air the way they once floated in the water that covered everything here.

I make it sound exotic, but the cliff is purely of local interest. I put too much of myself into the telling, always walking ahead of you. Come, we'll make our own path, not follow one trampled by my words.

On Skimming an Anthology of Contemporary American Poetry

My first impulse is to write a poem of my own, just as Olympic ice dancing makes me want to skate in an indoor arena. I know better than anyone where to touch my body, how to tighten long laces and leave earth, how to train on empty ice and prefer it. I skim in silence or to music, and when I pull off my skates I feel slow and heavy, the way I do when I come away from water.

Watching other skaters, I can't resist the sadness of the men or the joy of the women. My favorites are the ones who make difficult moves simply — perhaps I like them because they seem more alone.

Solitude and celebration. I'm covered with sweat. I wish someone would drop by ... a stranger who'd be excited to see me like this.

Stories from Life

I thought I was entitled to tell only one story, my story, until I heard yours. You told me about yourself in a way that made your story part of me, giving me two stories. One night I told them to a friend at a bar — she was sitting next to her husband, who was talking to someone on his other side, so she listened, and then she told me her story, and it made me richer. My face hurt, as it does when I smile and listen. I took our three stories to a party, and in telling them I mixed them up, and the stranger I was with grew excited and claimed to understand. We sat in a corner, and our time together seemed more than flirting. But, looking back, I think it was flirting. I was carried away like a person who wears jewels.

A Visit to the Grave

We dream — it is good we are dreaming —
—Emily Dickinson

I found I could push open the iron gate and come close enough to touch her, carrying with me my reluctance — I'd always been upset by her fragility, her many refusals. Next to her, I would feel much clumsier and stronger than I am.

In her presence my hesitation vanished, and I gripped her stone marker as I would the shoulders of a friend I wanted to surprise.

I gripped too hard — I might have hurt her. Ashamed, I left Amherst without visiting the house or tracing her steps in the garden, as I had hoped to do. It was my way of shielding us both from my need to belong.

That night I dropped my pride and met with her in a dream. We were alone at a table, my face and her skull. My face wanted to stop seeing, but by her gestures she made me feel that I was welcome, that I was meant to take the knife she offered and cut the white cake.

The Modern Wing

for Gail

After years of separation we stroll through the modern wing,
past paintings as foreign as neighborhoods we once cut
through. In an alcove we come upon a bucket and sponge
mop sculptured from paper — at first we think we've stumbled
into a cleaning closet! How strange to find these common tools
changed into art.

No one would guess we're related. In a painting I would
be the dark sister, you the blonde, our faces bent over a loom.
Not that I was a seamstress — I couldn't bear to gather and
hem loose fabric. When you first appeared in Mother's lap, so
serene and womanly even as an infant, I looked past you to
see what other disasters would come.

Those times I took my furious, agile body down the
sidewalk and into the woods, I must have been running away
from all those tiny stitches the machine's needle punched in. I
took the decorative pillows you made and pretended to
suffocate myself. I'm sorry I put you through that — I'm doing
better now. A closet of mops and brooms still troubles me, I
have difficulty accepting the cheerful aprons I'm given, and I
can't see paintings of corseted women without feeling the
terrible tightening. But I think I've stopped running away.

Earlier, when I first caught sight of you in the lobby, I felt the old impulse to hide. You wandered into the museum shop, and I spied on you. I pretended to look through the hanging tapestries, until finally I found the strength to look you in the face.

The Ideal Man

for Meredith

Conjure up your ideal man and study him with the same attention you once gave to Golden Books. He deserves a book all to himself, one painstakingly illuminated by a monk, but there is no time for that in this life. Instead, place his image against a dark curtain and imprint him in your mind, where not even the smallest scrap is lost. You don't want to lose your ideal man — you don't want to add to the drama.

You want him to lead a limited life. Restrict yourself to thinking about him only in movie theaters, before the lights dim. Give him a dwelling and a dressing gown. Adjust his blindfold. Protect yourself when he says he feels your presence deeply.

How, then, are you to satisfy the longing you feel now? What I'm going to suggest will seem strange. Think of each man you meet as part of you, perhaps a part you're dissatisfied with. When longing chokes you, you'll see a man holding out his arms. Know he is only part of you. Reach past him.

Tableau

At Easter the Congregational Church Men's Club put on a tableau of The Last Supper. Under a spotlight each disciple told about his character, and then together they assumed the pose of the famous painting. My uncle didn't say in his letter which part he played — not Jesus or Judas, I'm sure. As president and founder of the Men's Club, he'd take a more modest role. Not Doubting Thomas. One of the disciples chosen for loyalty, a willingness to believe.

I picture my aunt in the audience somewhere near the middle, spine straight, hands folded in her lap. She is resting her mind. Afterwards, she and other wives will pour coffee and wash up, wearing aprons they keep at the church.

Reunion

I was a best friend to God and Jesus. One year I won a pin
for perfect Sunday School attendance, and another year I
delivered the sermon on Youth Sunday, a sermon of reproach.
The adults in the congregation listened to my preaching with
the charitable misgivings owed, say, to a wedding sermon that
emphasizes will over sentiment.

There had been other Methodist preachers in my family,
two uncles, my grandfather, and even my father, who was not
ordained, but who often read the lesson. Perhaps, if I had been
a boy, I would have become a preacher — I certainly had the
earnestness for it.

I took that earnestness into womanhood and found myself
disliking God and Jesus — I couldn't stand their night sky
hanging over me like a man's umbrella. I left off praying,
except for the automatic prayer we breathe when frightened for
our children. I missed God and Jesus, the way you sometimes
miss the person you thought you had married. But I closed the
book they inhabited and let all the words about them wear the
pages thin.

Now, pictures of God and Jesus remind me of photos from
my high school yearbook. When I went to my 25th reunion
under a tent, they both were there. It was so good to see them

again — right away we got joking about that damp Sunrise Service at the reservoir, and the time Mr. LaVelle fell out of his swivel chair during the Lord's Prayer. Weak with the effort of laughing about memories, we sank cross-legged onto the carpet and drank toasts to one another from goblets set out for survivors.

Along for the Ride

for Carole

You're telling me about the funeral parlor in Florida that specializes in "natural settings" — for a price, Aunt Maude can be propped in the same swing where she spent so many happy hours. Or picture Uncle Bernie on the 9th green, visor shading his eyes. Children bent over a favorite toy, all signs of disease brushed away. Infants would be simplest, wrapped in flannel as though fresh from a bath.

We start inventing our own funerals — lashed to a raft on the rapids, drenched mourners lining the banks. Or, better still, slumped together in the basket of a rising balloon. I've never felt so alive.

Rescue

for Lynn

She's becoming more like herself, but her husband thinks she's turning into someone else. At night he leaves part of himself in her, but it doesn't stop her from changing a little more by morning.

In her dreams, the rose bushes are covered with beetles. Normally, she's not bothered by that sort of thing ... if there were only a few beetles she'd let them alone, but so many hooded bodies are swarming she thinks she'd better give the roses a chance.

Ode to the Female Impersonator

The bar quiets down. You come into the spotlight and start singing *Tea for Two*, the song my mother and father sang at the church variety show when I was ten. You balance a cup, the way they did, and you sing about the family you will raise, how happy you will be. The difference is, you play both parts, a baritone with cleavage. You really want this song to work.

I should get up there with you, I was an impersonator for so long. Women's clothing made me feel like a mannequin — one day in the dressing room I took off the taffeta gown for good and stood there in my panties and padded bra. I had breasts, but the saleslady thought I could use a little padding. The mirror told me to take off the bra and come closer.

Tea for Two was the only song my mother and father sang together. I remember sitting in the front row, finding it hard to believe that the actors on stage were my parents. The tablecloth was yellow and white check, and no place was set for me.

Prison Tour

In the old prisons of Paris, the women prisoners were allowed to wash their hair over a stone basin in the courtyard.

Because there is no women's prison in New Hampshire, women must be placed out-of-state, away from their children and any relatives who could fit in a visit. Women say New Hampshire needs a prison for them.

I like to think of the French women washing their hair in the courtyard, away from iron bars. I don't want to believe they were criminals.

New Hampshire women crowd into a communal shower far from home. I'm told some of them are cruel and violent — other women have told me this. It won't be easy for them to wash away their crimes, no matter how hard they soap every crevice.

As for the fugitives, the women who roam freely, we circle the prisons, we judge the height of the walls.

The Raft of Married People

I'm on a raft with other married men and women, carried along by a swift current. Some of the couples are praying — they are constant talkers. My husband and I sit back-to-back, supporting one another.

Onshore a woman comes into view. My husband sees her first and nudges me. Then I see her. She's undressing for a swim, paying no attention to hoots from some of the men. Now we are directly opposite, a stone's throw away. She's naked in water up to her knees, nipples erect from the cold. My breasts feel heavy. I nudge one of my nipples with the inside of my arm.

The raft plunges on, past cliffs on both sides. I find myself watching for a ledge, a stone shelf the size of a cot where I could lie down with a woman.

Different Mirrors

I have a true affection for the life I appear to lead — husband, two sons, a small town — it's the kind of life I foresaw as a child.

I feel affection for myself as well, for my wrists and ankles, my skin that shows traces of tanning, my face — I have great sympathy for my face. And for the animals we bring in. I watch them with the pleasure reserved for a special program on television.

If asked what's on my mind, I say, *I'm just thinking.* I think about the time I lived alone in the city and piled newspapers in the armchair. I wore a man's coat and smiled with half my mouth.

In those days, I never thought to buy mirrors for the apartments I lived in. Now I have a hand mirror a friend gave me, waist-high oval mirrors, all inherited, and a full-length mirror upstairs in my younger son's room. It was my gift to both of us — I catch sight of myself in a child's surroundings, the glass ripples slightly, and it's his turn.

A Shell Is Water that Has Stopped Moving

The sea increases my restlessness. I need the serenity a small lake has, her wheelbarrow of water.

The Great Lakes don't interest me, Lake Superior and the others rummaging in the heartland — of all bodies of water, they must be the least serene.

The lake I have in mind is surrounded by trees. A partially submerged shell glitters. I'm always glad to find shells in fresh water.

The lake I have in mind is inland. Some lakes are near the sea, but those may not be true lakes.

Last Illness

for Annie

I wish I lived near enough to see you often, to share your anguish as you watch your mother slip away. I'd bring you braided bread and carefully chosen gifts, like the handkerchiefs I used to buy to surprise my mother on her birthdays.

It was hard in those days to keep a secret. My little sister tagged along under her halo of blonde hair, and we asked Mother not to look. Then with our pooled allowances we selected the laciest handkerchief they had, white with embroidered roses.

Back at the revolving door, my sister said, "I'm not supposed to tell it's a handkerchief." I flew into a rage. That idiot gave away the whole thing!

"Don't worry," Mother soothed. "When the time comes, I won't remember."

The time comes, and she both remembers, and she doesn't … she remembers the love and forgets the rage.

Fear in a Public Place

Starting at the armpit, the doctor spirals around toward my nipple, pressing firmly with two fingers. He's looking for a lump that won't move, perhaps as small as a grain of sand. It seems hopeless, yet he won't stop.

Then, after a routine x-ray, I'm called back for another series. The left breast shows a suspicious shadow. Again I shoulder into the hospital rag called a gown. Again the technician lifts my breast onto the plate.

The crushing begins, a tank in a village of children. The prodigal slips under.

The Provinces of Sleep

Last night I dreamed a surgeon cut off my breasts — instead of nipples there were seams. I crossed the provinces of sleep looking for friends, someone I could tell, and I sobbed more deeply than I can when awake. Perhaps I only needed to lose one breast, perhaps the knife was too thorough.

This morning I held my breasts with relief. So much sorrow in one dream ... we find in sleep what we find in love.

Dying at Home

I cut purple and white lilacs to bring in closer. Your bed appears to quiver slightly, to float on an indiscernible current, the walls take on the grayish hue of a northern sky, and the floor becomes as marsh grass, slick and clumped. I sit in a chair next to you and prop my feet on the rung a few inches off the floor, balancing my hands on my knees as if sitting on a split rail fence. You're lying lengthwise on your fence. No matter how thin you are, there is not enough room for your body.

A Song for Dorothy

You were surrounded by friends, some visible, some as invisible as the memories running like spring water every which way.

One by one, we held your hands and tried to say goodbye. Our words fell short, until lifted by a current of music deep enough to carry their weight.

I sang to you, or, rather, I sang along with another singer who had a greater range. The song was written to someone of great beauty, meant to be sung to anyone, but especially to you. While we were singing, I risked looking up from the page.

You were tucked into your deathbed, each breath out a harsh sigh. I hope you could hear us. If not, I hope you brought the song with you, in case you might want to listen to it later.

Shadows

Every time you pick up a stone, you uncover a shadow. Here is the shadow of sad childhood times, here the shadow of a first marriage. Here is the deep shadow of envy. And here is the shadow of being born a woman, resting near the shadow of being born a man. Gather these shadows together, and you have an abyss.

You can make a shadow disappear — brush its shavings into a pile and sweep them away with your sleeve. When you were younger, did you ever pound a stone into powder? Pound a shadow into powder, using another shadow to do it. In the end, one last shadow slips across the moon, and you take the part of the crescent that shines.

These shadows can be thought of as shade. What is sadness, if not a time of balance? And, if you can't remember the joy this sadness balances, trust that it will come, that, for you, sadness is first.

POETRY FROM ALICE JAMES BOOKS